Light BASICS

a pattern collection
by Kerin Dimeler-Laurence

Copyright 2013 © Knit Picks

All rights reserved. This book or any portion thereof may not be reproduced or used in any manner whatsoever without the express written permission of the publisher except for the use of brief quotations in a book review.

Printed in the United States of America

Second Printing, 2017

ISBN 978-1-62767-003-6

Versa Press, Inc
800-447-7829

www.versapress.com

CONTENTS

Garter Ridge Hat — 6

Garter Stitch Shawlette — 10

Light Shell — 14

Light Tee — 20

Light Pullover — 28

Light Cardigan — 34

GARTER RIDGE HAT

by Kerin Dimeler-Laurence

FINISHED MEASUREMENTS
19" around (unstretched), 8.5-10.5" deep, or to desired depth

YARN
Knit Picks Stroll Hand Paint (75% Superwash Merino Wool, 25% Nylon; 462 yards/100g): Coffee Shop 25899, 1 hank.

NEEDLES
US 2 (3mm) DPNs and 16" circular needle, or longer circular needles for Magic Loop, or size to obtain gauge

NOTIONS
Yarn Needle
Stitch Markers

GAUGE
27 sts and 49 rows = 4" in Garter Ridge pattern in the round, blocked.

Garter Ridge Hat

This light and simple hat looks great in any fingering weight yarn and any color! Adding rows allows you to make this hat as short or slouchy as you like. The fabric is soft and stretchy and can accommodate a large range of head sizes.

Notes:

CDD (Centered Double Decrease)
Slip two stitches to the RH needle as if to K2tog. Knit the next stitch, then pass two slipped sts over; two sts removed.

Garter Ridge pattern (in the round)
Round 1: Knit.
Round 2: (P8, K1) around.

DIRECTIONS
Cast on 126 sts. PM and join to work in the round, being careful not to twist sts.

Begin working Garter Ridge pattern around the hat. Repeat these two rounds until the hat measures 6-9" long (6" will give a more beanie-like fit, while 9" or more will give a slouchy fit).

Crown Decreases
On the next round, begin decreasing for the crown.
Round 1: (K3, CDD, K3) around: 28 sts removed; 98 sts remain.
Round 2: (P6, K1) around.
Round 3: Knit.
Repeat Rounds 2 and 3 a total of five times (10 rounds), then repeat Round 2 once more.
Round 4: (K2, CDD, K2) around: 28 sts removed; 70 sts remain.
Round 5: (P4, K1) around.
Round 6: Knit.
Repeat Rounds 5 and 6 a total of four times (8 rounds), then repeat Round 5 once more.
Round 7: (K1, CDD, K1) around: 28 sts removed; 42 sts remain.
Round 8: (P2, K1) around.
Round 9: Knit.
Repeat Rounds 8 and 9 a total of three times (6 rounds), then Repeat round 8 once more.
Round 10: CDD around: 28 sts removed; 14 sts remain.
Round 11: Knit.
Round 12: K2tog around: 7 sts remain.

Break yarn, leaving a 12" tail. Pass the yarn tail through the remaining live sts and pull tight to close the hole. With a yarn needle, pull the tail through the center to the wrong side.

Finishing
Weave in ends. Wash and block to measurements.

GARTER SHAWLETTE

by Kerin Dimeler-Laurence

FINISHED MEASUREMENTS
Body of shawlette: 36" wingspan, 12" deep at center (not counting optional borders)

YARN
Knit Picks Stroll Tonal (75% Superwash Merino Wool, 25% Nylon; 462 yards/100g): Thunderhead 25386, 2 hanks.

NEEDLES
US 2 (3mm) 32" or longer circular needle, or size to obtain gauge

NOTIONS
Yarn Needle
Stitch Markers

GAUGE
26 sts and 52 rows = 4" in Garter stitch, blocked.

Garter Stitch Shawlette

Simple yarn overs add a lacy touch to the basic garter stitch shawlette. Spice up the edge with a simple lace pattern or a garter ridge pattern.

DIRECTIONS

Cast on 9 sts. Knit one row, marking center st.

Begin working Garter pattern:
Row 1: K2, YO, K to center st, YO, K1, YO, K to last 2 sts, YO, K2.
Row 2: K2, YO, K to last 2 sts, YO, K2.

Repeat rows 1 and 2 until shawlette measures 12" deep at the center point, ending by working Row 2.

Edging options

Lacy border
A simple lacy border can add a touch of class.
Worked over a multiple of 6 sts + 3
Row 1: K2, *YO, K1, CDD, K1, YO, K1; repeat from * to last st, K2.
Row 2: P2, *K5, P1; repeat from * to last st, P1.

Repeat these two rows for 3", or desired length. BO all sts loosely.

Garter Ridge pattern
Alternating between Stockinette and Garter stitch adds a simple, modern appeal.

Row 1: K2, YO, K to center st, YO, K1, YO, K to last 2 sts, YO, K2.
Row 2: P2, YO, P to last 2 sts, YO, P2.
Row 3: Repeat Row 1.
Row 4: Repeat Row 2.
Row 5: K2, YO, K to center st, YO, K1, YO, K to last 2 sts, YO, K2.
Row 6: K2, YO, K to last 2 sts, YO, K2.

Repeat these six rows three times, then repeat Rows 5 & 6 once more. BO all sts loosely.

Finishing

Weave in ends. Wash and block; pin out Garter st body of shawlette to the measurements given, and any edging beyond that measurement.

LIGHT BASIC SHELL

by Kerin Dimeler-Laurence

FINISHED MEASUREMENTS
32 (36, 40, 44, 48, 52, 56, 60, 64)" finished bust measurement

YARN
Knit Picks Stroll Glimmer (70% Fine Superwash Merino Wool, 25% Nylon, 5% Stellina; 231 yards/50g): Frost 25495, 3 (4, 4, 5, 6, 6, 7, 7, 8) balls.

NEEDLES
US 2 (3mm) 24-48" circular needles, or long circulars for Magic Loop, or size to obtain gauge

24-48" circular needles, or long circular needles for Magic Loop one size smaller than those used to obtain gauge
Spare DPNs in larger size for I-Cord

NOTIONS
Yarn Needle
Stitch Markers
Stitch Holders
Scrap Yarn for Provisional CO
Crochet Hook for Provisional CO

GAUGE
28 sts and 36 rows = 4" in St st on larger needles, blocked.

Light Basic Shell

This basic shell features turned hems and a scoop neck. The simple stockinette body and basic shaping allows you to embellish as you like.

Notes:
All references to *Right* and *Left* are as worn, unless otherwise noted.

Provisional Cast On (Crochet Chain method)
Using a crochet hook several sizes too big for the yarn, make a slipknot and chain for 1". Hold knitting needle in left hand. With yarn in back of the needle, work next chain st by pulling the yarn over the needle and through the chain st. Move yarn under and behind needle, and repeat for the number of sts required. Chain a few more sts off the needle, then break yarn and pull end through last chain. CO sts will be incorrectly mounted; knit into the back of these sts. To unravel (when sts need to be picked up), pull chain end out, and the chain should unravel, leaving live sts.

Join Hem
Unravel Provisional CO and place sts on spare needle. Hold these sts in back of the working needle, and work across row in pattern, working one st from front needle and one from the back K-wise together as one. This is worked like a Three-Needle Bind Off, without binding off.

M1L (Make 1 Left-leaning stitch):
PU the bar between st just worked and next st and place on LH needle mounted as a regular knit stitch; knit through the back of the loop.

M1R (Make 1 Right-leaning stitch):
PU the bar between st just worked and next st and place on LH needle backwards (incorrect stitch mount). Knit through the front of the loop.

Three-needle Bind Off
Hold the two pieces of knitting together with the points of the needles facing to the right. Insert a third needle into the first stitch on each of the needles knitwise, starting with the front needle. Work a knit stitch, pulling the loop through both of the stitches you've inserted the third needle through. After you've pulled the loop through, slip the first stitch off of each of the needles. This takes two stitches (one from the front needle and one from the back) and joins them to make one finished stitch on the third needle (held in your right hand). Repeat this motion, inserting your needle into one stitch on the front and back needles, knitting them together and slipping them off of the needles. Each time you complete a second stitch, pass the first finished stitch over the second and off of the needle (as you would in a traditional bind-off).

W&T (Wrap and Turn):
Work until the stitch to be wrapped. If knitting: bring yarn to the front of the work, slip next st as if to purl, return the yarn to the back; turn work and slip wrapped st onto RH needle. Continue across row. If purling: bring yarn to the back of the work, slip next st as if to purl, return the yarn to the front; turn work and slip wrapped st onto RH needle. Continue across row.

Picking up wraps: Work to the wrapped st. If knitting, insert the RH needle under the wrap(s), then through the wrapped st K-wise. Knit the wrap(s) together with the wrapped st. If Purling, slip the wrapped st P-wise onto the RH needle, and use the LH needle to lift the wrap(s) and place them on the RH needle. Slip wrap(s) and unworked st back to LH needle; purl all together through the back loop.

For video and photo tutorials for these and other techniques, visit www.knitpicks.com/wptutorials.

DIRECTIONS
Body
With smaller needles and scrap yarn, Provisionally CO 240 (268, 296, 328, 364, 384, 412, 444, 468). PM and join to work in the round, being careful not to twist sts. Attach Stroll and knit in St st for 9 rounds. Purl a turning round. Switch to larger needles and knit 8 rounds.

Unravel Provisional CO and place sts back on smaller needles. Join Hem (see instructions in *Notes* section).

Knit one round, placing marker after 120 (134, 148, 164, 182, 192, 206, 222, 234) sts to mark right underarm.

Shaping
Decrease Round: *K2, SSK, K to 4 sts before marker, K2tog, K2*, SM; repeat between *s around. 4 sts removed.

Increase Round: *K2, M1L, K to 2 sts before marker, M1R, K2*, SM; repeat between *s around. 4 sts increased.

The body will now be gently shaped up to the armholes.

Size 40: work a Decrease Round on the next round.

All sizes: Work a Decrease Round every 5th (5th, 5th, 5th, 6th, 7th, 7th, 8th) round 13 (14, 14, 15, 15, 13, 12, 12, 10) times.

52 (56, 60, 60, 60, 52, 48, 48, 40) sts removed; 188 (212, 236, 268, 304, 332, 364, 396, 428) sts total.

Work in plain Stockinette stitch for 6 (6, 8, 10, 16, 12, 8, 10, 14) rounds.

Work an Increase Round on the next round, then every 7th (6th, 6th, 6th, 8th, 7th, 8th, 9th, 12th) row 8 (9, 10, 9, 7, 7, 6, 5, 4) times. Work 9 (11, 6, 13, 9, 9, 10, 10, 8) rounds in St st. Place a locking stitch marker between the two center front stitches.

224 (252, 280, 308, 336, 364, 392, 420, 448) sts on the needles.

Armholes
On the next round, stitches are bound off at each armhole. After this, the Front and Back are worked flat separately to the shoulders. Note that Neckline instructions are worked at the same time as armholes; read both sections before continuing.

Work to 3 (3, 3, 3, 4, 6, 7, 6, 7) sts before the right underarm marker. BO the next 6 (6, 6, 6, 8, 12, 14, 12, 14) sts, removing marker. Repeat at left underarm marker. 106 (120, 134, 148, 160, 170, 182, 198, 210) sts remain across both Front and Back. Place Back sts on scrap yarn or a stitch holder, and work flat across front sts only.

Armhole Double Decrease Row:
RS: K3tog, K to last 3 sts, SSSK. 4 sts decreased.
WS: P3tog TBL, P to last 3 sts, P3tog. 4 sts decreased.

Armhole Decrease Row:
RS: K2tog, K to last 2 sts, SSK. 2 sts decreased.
WS: P2tog TBL, P to last 2 sts, P2tog. 2 sts decreased.

32: Work an Armhole Double Decrease Row, then work an Armhole Decrease Row, then work an Armhole Decrease Row every other row three times, then on the third row, then on the fifth row twice, then on the 12th row. 10 sts decreased on each side.

36: Work an Armhole Double Decrease Row, then work an Armhole Decrease Row every row four times, then every other row twice, then on the third row twice, then on the fourth row, then on the fifth row. 12 sts decreased on each side.

40: Work an Armhole Double Decrease Row every row twice, then work an Armhole Decrease Row every row five times, then every other row three times, then every third row twice, then on the fifth row. 15 sts decreased on each side.

44: Work an Armhole Double Decrease Row every row 3 times, then work an Armhole Decrease Row every row seven times, then every other row three times, then every third row twice, then on the fourth row, then on the fifth row. 20 sts decreased on each side.

48: Work an Armhole Double Decrease Row every row 5 times, then work an Armhole Decrease Row every row eight times, then every other row five times, then every fourth row twice. 25 sts decreased on each side.

52: Work an Armhole Double Decrease Row every row three times, then work an Armhole Decrease Row every row eight times, then every other row five times, then on the third row, then every fifth row twice. 22 sts decreased on each side.

56: Work an Armhole Double Decrease Row every row four times, then work an Armhole Decrease Row every row ten times, then every other row three times, then every third row three times, then on the fifth row. 25 sts decreased on each side.

60: Work an Armhole Double Decrease Row every row four times, then (work an Armhole Decrease Row, work an Armhole Double Decrease Row) twice, then work an Armhole Decrease Row every row nine times, then every other row three times, then every third row twice, then on the fourth row. 29 sts decreased on each side.

64: Work an Armhole Double Decrease Row every row five times, then (work an Armhole Decrease Row, work an Armhole Double Decrease Row) twice, then work an Armhole Decrease Row every row 11 times, then every other row three times, then every third row twice. 32 sts decreased on each side.

Continue across front in St st, following Neckline directions.

Neckline

The neckline begins while still working the Armhole decreases.

On the 14th (19th, 19th, 26th, 29th, 41st, 44th, 48th, 49th) row after the armhole bind off, work across to 3 sts before center front marker. BO the next 6 sts, removing marker. Continue to the end of the row, following armhole decrease instructions. On the next row, attach a new ball of yarn at the neckline edge across the gap, following decreases below, and work both sides together.

Neckline Double Decrease Row:
RS: K to last 3 sts of left neck edge, SSSK. K3tog, K across right shoulder. 4 sts decreased.
WS: P to last 3 sts of right neck edge, P3tog. P3tog TBL, P across left shoulder. 4 sts decreased.

Neckline Decrease Row:
RS: K to last 2 sts of left neck edge, SSK. K2tog, K across right shoulder. 2 sts decreased.
WS: P to last 2 sts of right neck edge, P2tog. P2tog TBL, P across left shoulder. 2 sts decreased.

Shape Neckline:
Work a Neckline Double Decrease Row every row 3 times; work a Neckline Decrease Row every row 7 times, then every other row 3 (3, 3, 3, 6, 6, 6, 6) times, then every third row 2 (4, 6, 6, 6, 8, 9, 9, 10) times. Then continue Neckline Decreases as follows:
32, 36: Work a Neckline Decrease Row every 6th row twice.
40: Work a Neckline Decrease Row on the next 6th row.
44: Work a Neckline Decrease Row every 4th row twice.
48: Work a Neckline Decrease Row every 4th row three times.

Work 11 (4, 7, 6, 2, 6, 2, 1, 0) rows in St st.

46 (50, 52, 54, 56, 60, 62, 62, 64) sts have been removed from the front; 20 (23, 26, 27, 27, 33, 35, 39, 41) sts remain on each shoulder.

Short rows
A set of short rows finishes off the shoulders.

On the next RS row, K to 6 (8, 9, 9, 7, 8, 9, 10, 10) sts before the end of the Right shoulder; Wrap & Turn. Purl back to 6 (8, 9, 9, 7, 8, 9, 10, 10) sts before the end of the Left shoulder; W&T. K to 6 (8, 9, 9, 7, 8, 9, 10, 10) sts before the wrapped st, W&T. P to 6 (8, 9, 9, 7, 8, 9, 10, 10) sts before the wrapped st, W&T. **Sizes 48, 52, 56, 60, 64:** Repeat the last two rows once more. Turn and knit across all sts, picking up wrapped sts and knitting them together with the sts they wrap.

Break yarn and put shoulders on st holders or scrap yarn.

Back

Place Back sts back on needles, and attach yarn ready to begin a RS row. Work through Armhole shaping directions as done for front. 86 (96, 104, 108, 110, 126, 132, 140, 146) sts remain.

Work 25 (40, 41, 40, 45, 48, 62, 64, 64) rows in St st.

On the next RS row, sts are bound off at the back neck to form the neckline.

K 21 (24, 27, 28, 28, 34, 36, 40, 42) sts, BO the next 44 (48, 50, 52, 54, 58, 60, 60, 62) sts, then K to the end of row.

Turn and P to 2 sts before neckline edge of left shoulder; P2tog. Attach a new ball of yarn at the right shoulder; P2tog TBL across the first 2 sts, then P to end. 20 (23, 26, 27, 27, 33, 35, 39, 41) sts remain on each shoulder.

Work short rows as done for front, reversing 'left' and 'right' notations, but do not break yarn.

Join Shoulders
Put front shoulder sts back on spare needles. Turn body inside out, and join the shoulders together using working yarn from the back and the Three-Needle Bind Off technique.

Finishing

Neckline and Armhole edges
Applied I-cord gives a clean edge to the neckline and armhole edges.

To work Applied I-cord:
With larger size DPNs, CO 3 sts.
*Knit two stitches and slip the third stitch knitwise.
PU and knit one more stitch from the edge. You will now have 4 stitches on your right needle.
Use your left needle tip to pass the slipped stitch over the last knitted stitch. This will leave you with three stitches on your right needle.
Slip these three stitches back onto the left needle tip, or slide to the other end of the needle, purlwise. Tug on the working yarn to tighten up the stitches.
Repeat these steps from *.

Starting at the center neckline and working first up the right neckline edge, use DPNs to work an I-cord around the neckline. When you have worked all the way around the neckline, break yarn and graft the live sts of the I-cord to the CO edge of the I-cord.

Starting at the bound off sts of the armhole, work an I-cord around each armhole. When you have worked all the way around the armhole, break yarn and graft the live sts of the I-cord to the CO edge of the I-cord.

Weave in ends. Wash and block to measurements.

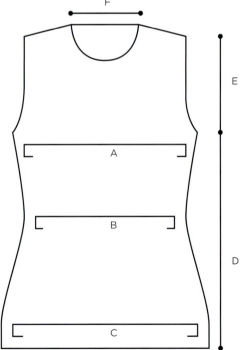

A: 32 (36, 40, 44, 48, 52, 56, 60, 64)"
B: 28 (32, 36, 40, 45, 48, 52, 57, 61)"
C: 34.25 (38.25, 42.25, 46.9, 52, 54.9, 58.9, 63.4, 66.9)"
D: 16 (16.3, 17.1, 17.7, 18, 17.9, 17.9, 17.9, 18.1)"
E: 6.5 (7, 7.3, 8.2, 8.6, 10.3, 10.5, 10.9, 11.1)"
F: 6.1 (6.6, 6.9, 7.2, 7.5, 8.1, 8.4, 8.4, 8.6)"

Light Basic Shell | 19

LIGHT BASIC TEE

by Kerin Dimeler-Laurence

FINISHED MEASUREMENTS
32 (36, 40, 44, 48, 52, 56, 60, 64)" finished bust measurement

YARN
Knit Picks Comfy Fingering (75% Pima Cotton, 25% Acrylic; 218 yards/50g): Marlin 24826, 4 (5, 5, 6, 7, 8, 8, 9, 9) balls.

NEEDLES
US 2 (3mm) 24-48" circular needles, and DPNs or long circulars for Magic Loop, or size to obtain gauge
24-48" circular needles, and DPNs or long circular needles for Magic Loop one size smaller than those used to obtain gauge
Spare DPNs in larger size for I-Cord

NOTIONS
Yarn Needle
Stitch Markers
Stitch Holders
Scrap Yarn for Provisional CO
Crochet Hook for Provisional CO

GAUGE
28 sts and 36 rows = 4" in St st on larger needles, blocked.

Light Basic Tee

This simple tee features basic hems and a curved v-neck. The simple stockinette body and basic shaping allows you to embellish as you like.

Notes:

All references to *Right* and *Left* are as worn, unless otherwise noted.

Provisional Cast On (Crochet Chain method)

Using a crochet hook several sizes too big for the yarn, make a slipknot and chain for 1". Hold knitting needle in left hand. With yarn in back of the needle, work next chain st by pulling the yarn over the needle and through the chain st. Move yarn under and behind needle, and repeat for the number of sts required. Chain a few more sts off the needle, then break yarn and pull end through last chain. CO sts will be incorrectly mounted; knit into the back of these sts. To unravel (when sts need to be picked up), pull chain end out, and the chain should unravel, leaving live sts.

Join Hem

Unravel Provisional CO and place sts on spare needle. Hold these sts in back of the working needle, and work across row in pattern, working one st from front needle and one from the back K-wise together as one. This is worked like a Three-Needle Bind Off, without binding off.

M1L (Make 1 Left-leaning stitch):
PU the bar between st just worked and next st and place on LH needle mounted as a regular knit stitch; knit through the back of the loop.

M1R (Make 1 Right-leaning stitch):
PU the bar between st just worked and next st and place on LH needle backwards (incorrect stitch mount). Knit through the front of the loop.

Three-Needle Bind Off

Hold the two pieces of knitting together with the points of the needles facing to the right. Insert a third needle into the first stitch on each of the needles knitwise, starting with the front needle. Work a knit stitch, pulling the loop through both of the stitches you've inserted the third needle through. After you've pulled the loop through, slip the first stitch off of each of the needles. This takes two stitches (one from the front needle and one from the back) and joins them to make one finished stitch on the third needle (held in your right hand). Repeat this motion, inserting your needle into one stitch on the front and back needles, knitting them together and slipping them off of the needles. Each time you complete a second stitch, pass the first finished stitch over the second and off of the needle (as you would in a traditional bind-off).

W&T (Wrap and Turn):

Work until the stitch to be wrapped. If knitting: bring yarn to the front of the work, slip next st as if to purl, return the yarn to the back; turn work and slip wrapped st onto RH needle. Continue across row. If purling: bring yarn to the back of the work, slip next st as if to purl, return the yarn to the front; turn work and slip wrapped st onto RH needle. Continue across row.

Picking up wraps: Work to the wrapped st. If knitting, insert the RH needle under the wrap(s), then through the wrapped st K-wise. Knit the wrap(s) together with the wrapped st. If Purling, slip the wrapped st P-wise onto the RH needle, and use the LH needle to lift the wrap(s) and place them on the RH needle. Slip wrap(s) and unworked st back to LH needle; purl all together through the back loop.

For video and photo tutorials for these and other techniques, visit www.knitpicks.com/wptutorials.

DIRECTIONS

Sleeves

The sleeves begin above the elbow with a turned hem and are increased to the underarm. Make two identical sleeves.

With smaller needles and scrap yarn, Provisionally CO 80 (86, 92, 98, 112, 124, 136, 146, 152) sts. PM and join to work in the round, being careful not to twist sts. Attach Comfy and knit in St st for 5 rounds. Purl a turning round. Switch to larger needles and knit 5 rounds.

Unravel Provisional CO and place sts back on smaller needles. Join Hem (see instructions in *Notes* section).

Sleeve Increases

From here, the sleeves are lightly increased to the underarms.

Increase Round: K1, M1L, K to last st, M1R, K1. 2 sts increased.

Sizes 40, 44, 52, 56: work an Increase Round on the first round. **Size 60:** Work an Increase Round on the first and third rounds.

All sizes: work an Increase Round every 13th (8th, 6th, 6th, 5th, 4th, 4th, 3rd, 3rd) round 2 (4, 4, 4, 5, 6, 6, 10, 10) times. Knit 0 (2, 2, 2, 3, 4, 4, 0, 0) rounds plain.

84 (94, 102, 108, 122, 138, 150, 170, 172) sts on the needles.

Sleeve Cap Shaping

On the next round, stitches are bound off at the base of the sleeve cap. The cap is then worked flat (back and forth) to the end.

Work to 5 (5, 8, 6, 7, 8, 5, 5, 9) sts before the end of the round. BO the last 5 (5, 8, 6, 7, 8, 5, 5, 9) sts of the round, then the first 7 (7, 10, 8, 9, 10, 7, 7, 11) sts of the next round. Knit to the last 3 sts of the row, SSSK. You are now working flat. 70 (80, 82, 92, 104, 118, 136, 156, 150) sts remain.

Shape the caps as follows. For these directions, references to *left* and *right* are as-oriented; *right* is the beginning of a row, and *left* is the end of a row. Knit directions are for RS rows and purl directions are for WS rows.

Double Decrease Row: K3tog or P3tog TBL over the first three sts at *right* edge; SSSK or P3tog over last three sts at *left* edge. 2 sts removed at each edge.

Decrease Row: K2tog or P2tog TBL over the first two sts at *right* edge; SSK or P2tog over last two sts at *left* edge. 1 st removed at each edge.

32: Work a Double Decrease Row on the next row; work a Decrease Row every row three times, then every other row eight times, then every third row three times, then every other row three times, then every row five times; work a Double Decrease Row. 52 sts decreased; 18 sts remain.

36: Work a Double Decrease Row on the next 2 rows; work a Decrease Row every row six times, then every other row 11 times, then every row four times; work a Double Decrease Row every row three times. 62 sts decreased; 18 sts remain.

40: Work a Double Decrease Row on the next two rows; work a Decrease Row every row six times, then every other row seven times, then every third row twice, then every other row four times, then every row four times; work a Double Decrease Row every row twice. 62 sts decreased; 20 sts remain.

44: Work a Double Decrease Row on the next two rows; work a Decrease Row every row seven times, then every other row five times, then every third row five times, then every other row four times, then every row four times; work a Double Decrease Row every row three times. 70 sts decreased; 22 sts remain.

48: Work a Double Decrease Row every row four times; work a Decrease Row every row four times, then every other row eight times, then every third row three times, then every other row five times, then every row six times; work a Double Decrease Row every row three times. 80 sts decreased; 24 sts remain.

52: Work a Double Decrease Row every row four times; work a Decrease Row every row six times, then every other row seven times, then every third row four times, then every other row seven times, then every row five times; work a Double Decrease Row every row four times. 90 sts decreased; 28 sts remain.

56: Work a Double Decrease Row every row six times; work a Decrease Row every row nine times, then every other row 17 times, then every row three times; work a Double Decrease Row every row seven times. 110 sts decreased; 26 sts remain.

60: Work a Double Decrease Row every row seven times; work a Decrease Row every row 12 times, then every other row 16 times, then every row four times; work a Double Decrease Row every row seven times. 120 sts decreased; 36 sts remain.

64: Work a Double Decrease Row every row seven times; (work a Decrease Row, Work a Double Decrease Row) twice, work a Decrease Row every row seven times, then every other row five times, then every third row three times, then every other row five times, then every row seven times; work a Double Decrease Row every row five times. 114 sts decreased; 36 sts remain.

After the last row of the Sleeve Cap, BO all sts.

Make a second sleeve the same way.

Body

The body begins with the same basic hem as the sleeves.

With smaller needles and scrap yarn, Provisionally CO 240 (268, 296, 328, 364, 384, 412, 444, 468). PM and join to work in the round, being careful not to twist sts. Attach Comfy and knit in St st for 9 rounds. Purl a turning round. Switch to larger needles and knit 8 rounds, placing marker after 120 (134, 148, 164, 182, 192, 206, 222, 234) sts on the last round to mark right underarm.

Unravel Provisional CO and place sts back on smaller needles. Join Hem (see instructions in *Notes* section).

Shaping

Decrease Round: *K2, SSK, K to 4 sts before marker, K2tog, K2*, SM; repeat between *s around. 4 sts removed.

Increase Round: *K2, M1L, K to 2 sts before marker, M1R, K2*, SM; repeat between *s around. 4 sts increased.

The body will now be gently shaped up to the armholes.

Size 40: work a Decrease Round on the next round.

All sizes: Work a Decrease Round every 5th (5th, 5th, 5th, 5th, 6th, 7th, 7th, 8th) round 13 (14, 14, 15, 15, 13, 12, 12, 10) times.

52 (56, 60, 60, 60, 52, 48, 48, 40) sts removed; 188 (212, 236, 268, 304, 332, 364, 396, 428) sts total.

Work in plain Stockinette stitch for 6 (6, 8, 10, 16, 12, 8, 10, 14) rounds.

Work an Increase Round on the next round, then every 7th (6th, 6th, 6th, 8th, 7th, 8th, 9th, 12th) row 8 (9, 10, 9, 7, 7, 6, 5, 4) times. Work 5 (7, 1, 7, 3, 3, 3, 3, 0) rounds in St st. Place a locking stitch marker between the two center front stitches.

224 (252, 280, 308, 336, 364, 392, 420, 448) sts on the needles.

Armholes

On the next round, stitches are bound off at each armhole. After this, the Front and Back are worked flat separately to the shoulders. Note that Neckline instructions are worked at the same time as armholes; read both sections before continuing.

Work to 4 (4, 4, 4, 5, 8, 9, 7, 9) sts before the right underarm marker. BO the next 8 (8, 8, 8, 10, 16, 18, 14, 18) sts, removing marker. Repeat at left underarm marker. 104 (118, 132, 146, 158, 166, 178, 196, 206) sts remain across both Front and Back. Place Back sts on scrap yarn or a stitch holder, and work flat across front sts only.

Armhole Double Decrease Row:
RS: K3tog, K to last 3 sts, SSSK. 4 sts decreased.
WS: P3tog TBL, P to last 3 sts, P3tog. 4 sts decreased.

Armhole Decrease Row:
RS: K2tog, K to last 2 sts, SSK. 2 sts decreased.
WS: P2tog TBL, P to last 2 sts, P2tog. 2 sts decreased.

32: Work an Armhole Double Decrease Row, then work an Armhole Decrease Row, then work an Armhole Decrease Row every other row three times, then on the third row, then on the fifth row twice, then on the 12th row. 10 sts decreased on each side.

36: Work an Armhole Double Decrease Row, then work an Armhole Decrease Row every row four times, then every other row twice, then on the third row twice, then on the fourth row, then on the fifth row. 12 sts decreased on each side.

40: Work an Armhole Double Decrease Row every row twice, then work an Armhole Decrease Row every row five times, then every other row three times, then every third row twice, then on the fifth row. 15 sts decreased on each side.

44: Work an Armhole Double Decrease Row every row 3 times, then work an Armhole Decrease Row every row seven times, then every other row three times, then every third row twice, then on the fourth row, then on the fifth row. 20 sts decreased on each side.

48: Work an Armhole Double Decrease Row every row 5 times, then work an Armhole Decrease Row every row eight times, then every other row five times, then every fourth row twice. 25 sts decreased on each side.

52: Work an Armhole Double Decrease Row every row three times, then work an Armhole Decrease Row every row eight times, then every other row five times, then on the third row, then every fifth row twice. 22 sts decreased on each side.

56: Work an Armhole Double Decrease Row every row four times, then work an Armhole Decrease Row every row ten times, then every other row three times, then every third row three times, then on the fifth row. 25 sts decreased on each side.

60: Work an Armhole Double Decrease Row every row four times, then (work an Armhole Decrease Row, work an Armhole Double Decrease Row) twice, then work an Armhole Decrease Row every row nine times, then every other row three times, then every third row twice, then on the fourth row. 29 sts decreased on each side;

64: Work an Armhole Double Decrease Row every row five times, then (work an Armhole Decrease Row, work an Armhole Double Decrease Row) twice, then work an Armhole Decrease Row every row 11 times, then every other row three times, then every third row twice. 32 sts decreased on each side.

Neckline
The neckline begins while still working the Armhole decreases. On the 10th (13th, 15th, 20th, 23rd, 35th, 36th, 36th, 38th) row after the armhole bind off, work across to 1 st before center front marker. BO the next 2 sts, removing marker. Continue to the end of the row, following armhole decrease instructions. On the next row, attach a new ball of yarn at the neckline edge across the gap, following decreases below, and work both sides together.

Neckline Decrease Row:
RS: K to last 2 sts of left neck edge, SSK. K2tog, K across right shoulder.
WS: P to last 2 sts of right neck edge, P2tog. P2tog TBL, P across left shoulder.

24 | Light Basic Tee

Shape Neckline:
Work a Neckline Decrease Row every row 4 (4, 4, 4, 4, 5, 5, 6) times, then every other row 5 (5, 5, 5, 9, 9, 9, 9) times, then every third row 4 (4, 9, 9, 9, 7, 7, 7, 7) times, then every fourth row 2 (3, 2, 2, 2, 3, 3, 3, 3) times. Then continue Neckline Decreases as follows:
32: Work a Neckline Decrease Row on the next 8th row, then the next 11th row.
36: Work a Neckline Decrease Row every 6th row twice.
40: Work 7 rows in St st.
44: Work a Neckline Decrease Row on the next 6th row.
48: Work a Neckline Decrease Row every 6th row twice.
52, 56, 60, 64: Work a Neckline Decrease Row every 5th row twice.

Work 3 (6, 9, 6, 1, 10, 3, 3, 2) rows in St st.

36 (38, 42, 44, 46, 52, 54, 54, 56) sts have been removed from the front; 24 (28, 30, 31, 31, 35, 37, 42, 43) sts remain on each shoulder.

Short rows
A set of short rows finishes off the shoulders.

On the next RS row, K to 8 (9, 10, 10, 7, 8, 9, 10, 10) sts before the end of the Right shoulder; Wrap & Turn. Purl back to 8 (9, 10, 10, 7, 8, 9, 10, 10) sts before the end of the Left shoulder; W&T. K to 8 (9, 10, 10, 7, 8, 9, 10, 10) sts before the wrapped st, W&T. P to 8 (9, 10, 10, 7, 8, 9, 10, 10) sts before the wrapped st, W&T. **Sizes 48, 52, 56, 60, 64**: repeat the last two rows once more. Turn and knit across all sts, picking up wrapped sts and knitting them together with the sts they wrap.

Break yarn and put shoulders on st holders or scrap yarn.

Back
Place Back sts back on needles, and attach yarn ready to begin a RS row. Work through Armhole shaping directions as done for front. 84 (94, 102, 106, 108, 122, 128, 138, 142) sts remain.

Work 29 (44, 46, 45, 51, 54, 69, 71, 72) rows in St st.

On the next RS row, sts are bound off at the back neck to form the neckline.

K 26 (28, 30, 31, 31, 35, 37, 42, 43) sts, BO the next 36 (38, 42, 44, 46, 52, 54, 54, 56) sts, then K to the end of row.

Turn and P to 2 sts before neckline edge of left shoulder; P2tog. Attach a new ball of yarn at the right shoulder; P2tog TBL across the first 2 sts, then P to end. 24 (27, 30, 31, 31, 35, 37, 42, 43) sts remain on each shoulder.

Work short rows as done for front, reversing 'right' and 'left' notations, but do not break yarn.

Join Shoulders
Turn body inside out, and join the shoulders together using working yarn from the back and the 3-needle Bind-Off technique.

Finishing
Set in Sleeves
With right sides facing out, set sleeves into armhole openings, making sure that the center of each sleeve cap is placed at the shoulder seam and that the seam under the sleeve and bound off sts of the armhole are centered. Pin in place. Using yarn needle and yarn, begin at the underarm and sew sleeves into the armholes, using Mattress stitch.

Applied I-cord Neckline
Applied I-cord gives a clean edge to the neckline. Starting at the center neckline and working first up the right neckline edge, use smaller DPNs to work an I-cord around the neckline.

To work Applied I-cord:
CO 3 sts.
*Knit two stitches and slip the third stitch knitwise.
PU and knit one more stitch from the edge. You will now have 4 stitches on your right needle.
Use your left needle tip to pass the slipped stitch over the last knitted stitch. This will leave you with three stitches on your right needle.
Slip these three stitches back onto the left needle tip, or slide to the other end of the needle, purlwise. Tug on the working yarn to tighten up the stitches.
Repeat these steps from *.

When you have worked all the way around the neckline, break yarn and graft the live sts of the I-cord to the CO edge of the I-cord.

Weave in ends. Wash and block to measurements.

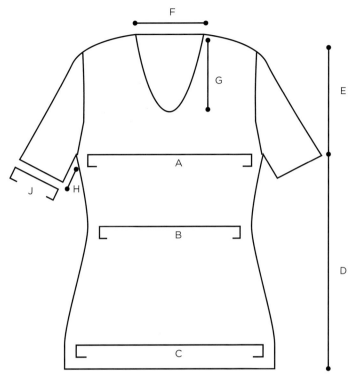

A: 32 (36, 40, 44, 48, 52, 56, 60, 64)"
B: 28 (32, 36, 40, 45, 48, 52, 57, 61)"
C: 34.25 (38.25, 42.25, 46.9, 52, 54.9, 58.9, 63.4, 66.9)"
D: 16 (16.7, 16.8, 17.3, 17.7, 17.6, 17.2, 17.3, 17.4)"
E: 7 (7.4, 7.9, 8.8, 9.2, 11, 11.6, 11.7, 12)"
F: 4.6 (5.2, 5.5, 5.8, 6.1, 6.9, 7.2, 7.2, 7.5)"
G: 6.7 (6.7, 6.9, 7.2, 7.6, 8.1, 8.3, 8.3, 8.3)"
H: 3.6 (3.6, 3.6, 3.6, 3.8, 3.8, 3.8, 4, 4)"
J: 8.9 (9.6, 10.2, 10.9, 12.4, 13.8, 15.1, 16.2, 16.9)"

LIGHT BASIC PULLOVER

by Kerin Dimeler-Laurence

Finished Measurements
33 (37, 41, 45, 49, 53, 57, 61, 65)" finished bust measurement

Yarn
Knit Picks Capretta (80% Fine Merino Wool, 10% Cashmere, 10% Nylon; 230 yards/50g): Cream 25600, 6 (6, 7, 8, 9, 9, 10, 11, 11) balls.

Needles
US 2 (3mm) DPNs and 24-48" circular needles, or long circulars for Magic Loop, or size to obtain gauge

DPNs and 24-48" circular needles, or long circular needles for Magic Loop two sizes smaller than those used to obtain gauge

Notions
Yarn Needle
Stitch Markers
Stitch Holders or Scrap Yarn

Gauge
28 sts and 36 rows = 4" in St st, blocked.

Light Basic Pullover

This simple pullover features basic ribbed cuffs and the options for a crew or turtleneck. The simple stockinette body and basic shaping allows you to embellish as you like.

Notes:
All references to *Right* and *Left* are as worn, unless otherwise noted.

M1L (Make 1 Left-leaning stitch): PU the bar between st just worked and next st and place on LH needle mounted as a regular knit stitch; knit through the back of the loop.

M1R (Make 1 Right-leaning stitch): PU the bar between st just worked and next st and place on LH needle backwards (incorrect stitch mount). Knit through the front of the loop.

Three Needle Bind Off
Hold the two pieces of knitting together with the points of the needles facing to the right. Insert a third needle into the first stitch on each of the needles knitwise, starting with the front needle. Work a knit stitch, pulling the loop through both of the stitches you've inserted the third needle through. After you've pulled the loop through, slip the first stitch off of each of the needles. This takes two stitches (one from the front needle and one from the back) and joins them to make one finished stitch on the third needle (held in your right hand). Repeat this motion, inserting your needle into one stitch on the front and back needles, knitting them together and slipping them off of the needles. Each time you complete a second stitch, pass the first finished stitch over the second and off of the needle (as you would in a traditional bind-off).

W&T (Wrap and Turn):
Work until the stitch to be wrapped. If knitting: bring yarn to the front of the work, slip next st as if to purl, return the yarn to the back; turn work and slip wrapped st onto RH needle. Continue across row. If purling: bring yarn to the back of the work, slip next st as if to purl, return the yarn to the front; turn work and slip wrapped st onto RH needle. Continue across row.

Picking up wraps: Work to the wrapped st. If knitting, insert the RH needle under the wrap(s), then through the wrapped st K-wise. Knit the wrap(s) together with the wrapped st. If Purling, slip the wrapped st P-wise onto the RH needle, and use the LH needle to lift the wrap(s) and place them on the RH needle. Slip wrap(s) and unworked st back to LH needle; purl all together through the back loop.

For video and photo tutorials for these and other techniques, visit www.knitpicks.com/wptutorials.

DIRECTIONS
Sleeves

The sleeves begin at the wrist and are increased to the underarm. Make two identical sleeves.

With smaller needles, CO 52 (56, 60, 66, 70, 78, 84, 86, 88) sts. PM and join to work in the round, being careful not to twist sts. Work in K1, P1 rib for 2". Switch to larger needles.

Sleeve Increases
From here, the sleeves are lightly increased to the underarms.

Increase Round: K1, M1L, K to last st, M1R, K1. 2 sts increased.

Sizes 41, 45, 53, 57: work an Increase Round on the first round.
Size 61: Work an Increase Round on the first and third rounds.

All sizes: work an Increase Round every 9th (8th, 8th, 8th, 6th, 5th and 11th, 5th, 4th, 3rd and 7th) round 16 (19, 19, 19, 26, 14, 31, 38, 21) times. Knit 6 (0, 1, 1, 0, 1, 0, 3, 5) rounds plain.

84 (94, 100, 106, 122, 136, 148, 166, 172) sts on the needles.

Sleeve Cap Shaping
On the next round, stitches are bound off at the base of the sleeve cap. The cap is then worked flat (back and forth) to the end.

Work to 5 (5, 8, 6, 7, 8, 5, 5, 9) sts before the end of the round. BO the last 5 (5, 8, 6, 7, 8, 5, 5, 9) sts of the round, then the first 7 (7, 10, 8, 9, 10, 7, 7, 11) sts of the next round. Knit to the last 3 sts of the row, SSSK. You are now working flat. 70 (80, 80, 90, 104, 116, 134, 152, 150) sts remain.

Shape the caps as follows. For these directions, references to *left* and *right* are as-oriented; *right* is the beginning of a row, and *left* is the end of a row. Knit directions are for RS rows and purl directions are for WS rows.

Double Decrease Row: K3tog or P3tog TBL over the first three sts at *right* edge; SSSK or P3tog over last three sts at *left* edge. 2 sts removed at each edge.

Decrease Row: K2tog or P2tog TBL over the first two sts at *right* edge; SSK or P2tog over last two sts at *left* edge. 1 st removed at each edge.

33: Work a Double Decrease Row on the next row; work a Decrease Row every row three times, then every other row eight times, then every third row three times, then every other row three times, then every row five times; work a Double Decrease. 52 sts decreased; 18 sts remain.

37: Work a Double Decrease Row on the next 2 rows; work a Decrease Row every row six times, then every other row 12 times, then every row four times; work a Double Decrease Row every row three times. 64 sts decreased; 16 sts remain.

41: Work a Double Decrease Row on the next row; work a Decrease Row every row six times, then every other row seven times, then every third row twice, then every other row four times, then every row four times; work a Double Decrease Row every row twice. 58 sts decreased; 22 sts remain.

45: Work a Double Decrease Row every row twice; work a Decrease Row every row seven times, then every other row five times, then every third row five times, then every other row four times, then every row four times; work a Double Decrease Row every row three times. 70 sts decreased; 20 sts remain.

49: Work a Double Decrease Row every row four times; work a Decrease Row every row four times, then every other row eight times, then every third row three times, then every other row five times, then every row six times; work a Double Decrease Row every row three times. 80 sts decreased; 24 sts remain.

53: Work a Double Decrease Row every row four times; work a Decrease Row every row six times, then every other row seven times, then every third row four times, then every other row seven times, then every row five times; work a Double Decrease Row every row four times. 90 sts decreased; 26 sts remain.

57: Work a Double Decrease Row every row six times; work a Decrease Row every row nine times, then every other row 17 times, then every row three times; work a Double Decrease Row every row seven times. 110 sts decreased; 24 sts remain.

61: Work a Double Decrease Row every row seven times; work a Decrease Row every row 12 times, then every other row 16 times, then every row four times; work a Double Decrease Row every row seven times. 120 sts decreased; 36 sts remain.

65: Work a Double Decrease Row every row seven times; (work a Decrease Row, Work a Double Decrease Row) twice, work a Decrease Row every row seven times, then every other row five times, then every third row three times, then every other row six times, then every row seven times; work a Double Decrease Row every row five times. 114 sts decreased; 36 sts remain.

After the last row of the Sleeve Cap, BO all sts.

Make a second sleeve the same way.

Body

The body begins with the same ribbing as the sleeves.

With smaller needles, CO 240 (268, 296, 328, 364, 384, 412, 444, 468). PM and join to work in the round, being careful not to twist sts. Work in K1, P1 rib for 2" or desired depth. Switch to larger needles.

Knit one round, placing marker after 120 (134, 148, 164, 182, 192, 206, 222, 234) sts to mark right underarm.

Shaping

Decrease Round: *K2, SSK, K to 4 sts before marker, K2tog, K2*, SM; repeat between *s around. 4 sts removed.

Increase Round: *K2, M1L, K to 2 sts before marker, M1R, K2*, SM; repeat between *s around. 4 sts increased.

The body will now be gently shaped up to the armholes.

Work a Decrease Round every 7th (7th, 6th, 7th, 9th, 10th, 10th, 9th, 9th) round 9 (9, 12, 11, 9, 8, 8, 9, 9) times.

Size 37: Work a Decrease Round on the next 4th round.

36 (40, 48, 44, 36, 32, 32, 36, 36) sts removed; 204 (228, 248, 284, 328, 352, 380, 408, 432) sts total.

Work in plain Stockinette stitch for 8 (8, 8, 8, 10, 10, 12, 13, 13) rounds.

Work an Increase Round on the next round, then every 10th (9th, 7th, 9th, 20th, 13th, 13th, 12th, 10th) row 6 (7, 9, 7, 3, 4, 4, 4, 5) times.

232 (260, 288, 316, 344, 372, 400, 428, 456) sts on the needles.

Armholes

On the next round, stitches are bound off at each armhole.

After this, the Front and Back are worked flat separately to the shoulders.

Work to 4 (4, 4, 4, 5, 8, 9, 7, 9) sts before the right underarm marker. BO the next 8 (8, 8, 8, 10, 16, 18, 14, 18) sts, removing marker. Repeat at left underarm marker. 108 (122, 136, 150, 162, 170, 182, 200, 210) sts remain across both Front and Back. Place Back sts on scrap yarn or a stitch holder, and work flat across front sts only.

Armhole Double Decrease Row:
RS: K3tog, K to last 3 sts, SSSK. 4 sts decreased.
WS: P3tog TBL, P to last 3 sts, P3tog. 4 sts decreased.

Armhole Decrease Row:
RS: K2tog, K to last 2 sts, SSK. 2 sts decreased.
WS: P2tog TBL, P to last 2 sts, P2tog. 2 sts decreased.

33: Work an Armhole Double Decrease Row, then work an Armhole Decrease Row, then work an Armhole Decrease Row every other row three times, then on the third row, then on the fifth row twice, then on the 12th row. 10 sts decreased on each side; 88 sts remain across front. Work 4 rows plain.

37: Work an Armhole Double Decrease Row, then work an Armhole Decrease Row every row four times, then every other row twice, then on the third row twice, then on the fourth row, then on the fifth row. 12 sts decreased on each side; 98 sts remain across front. Work 20 rows plain.

41: Work an Armhole Double Decrease Row every row twice, then work an Armhole Decrease Row every row five times, then every other row three times, then every third row twice, then on the fifth row. 15 sts decreased on each side; 106 sts remain across front. Work 20 rows plain.

45: Work an Armhole Double Decrease Row every row 3 times, then work an Armhole Decrease Row every row seven times, then every other row three times, then every third row twice, then on the fourth row, then on the fifth row. 20 sts decreased on each side; 110 sts remain across front. Work 19 rows plain.

49: Work an Armhole Double Decrease Row every row 5 times, then work an Armhole Decrease Row every row eight times, then every other row five times, then every fourth row twice. 25 sts decreased on each side; 112 sts remain across front. Work 25 rows plain.

53: Work an Armhole Double Decrease Row every row three times, then work an Armhole Decrease Row every row eight times, then every other row five times, then on the third row, then every fifth row twice. 22 sts decreased on each side; 126 sts remain across front. Work 25 rows plain.

57: Work an Armhole Double Decrease Row every row four times, then work an Armhole Decrease Row every row ten times, then every other row three times, then every third row three times, then on the fifth row. 25 sts decreased on each side; 132 sts remain across front. Work 38 rows plain.

61: Work an Armhole Double Decrease Row every row four times, then (work an Armhole Decrease Row, work an Armhole Double Decrease Row) twice, then work an Armhole Decrease Row every row nine times, then every other row three times, then every third row twice, then on the fourth row. 29 sts decreased on each side; 142 sts remain across front. Work 43 rows plain.

65: Work an Armhole Double Decrease Row every row five times, then (work an Armhole Decrease Row, work an Armhole Double Decrease Row) twice, then work an Armhole Decrease Row every row 11 times, then every other row three times, then every third row twice. 32 sts decreased on each side; 146 sts remain across front. Work 45 rows plain.

Neckline
On the next RS row, sts are bound off at the front neck to form the neckline.

Knit 39 (44, 48, 49, 49, 53, 56, 61, 63) sts, BO the next 10 (10, 10, 12, 14, 20, 20, 20, 20) sts; K to end. Follow neckline decrease directions below; attach a second ball of yarn at the left neckline edge and work both sides of the neckline together.

Neckline Double Decrease Row:
RS: K to last 3 sts of left neck edge, SSSK. K3tog, K across right shoulder. 4 sts decreased.
WS: P to last 3 sts of right neck edge, P3tog. P3tog TBL, P across left shoulder. 4 sts decreased.

Neckline Decrease Row:
RS: K to last 2 sts of left neck edge, SSK. K2tog, K across right shoulder. 2 sts decreased.
WS: P to last 2 sts of right neck edge, P2tog. P2tog TBL, P across left shoulder. 2 sts decreased.

Shape Neckline:
Work a Neckline Double Decrease Row every row 5 (5, 5, 5, 5, 5, 5, 4, 4) times, then (work a Neckline Decrease Row, then a Neckline Double Decrease Row) 1 (1, 1, 1, 2, 2, 2, 2) times, then work a Neckline Decrease Row every row 3 times, then every other row 3, (3, 3, 3, 3, 2, 2, 3, 3) times, then every third row 2 (2, 3, 3, 3, 1, 2, 3, 3) times Work 2 (1, 0, 0, 0, 9, 7, 6, 6) rows in plain St st. 21 (21, 22, 22, 22, 22, 23, 23, 23) sts have been removed from each front; 18 (23, 26, 27, 27, 31, 33, 38, 40) sts remain on each.

Short rows
A set of short rows finishes off the shoulders.

On the next RS row, K to 6 (7, 8, 8, 7, 8, 8, 10, 10) sts before the end of the Right shoulder; Wrap & Turn. Purl back to 6 (7, 8, 8, 7, 8, 8, 10, 10) sts before the end of the Left shoulder; W&T. K to 6 (7, 8, 8, 7, 8, 8, 10, 10) sts before the wrapped st, W&T. P to 6 (7, 8, 8, 7, 8, 8, 10, 10) sts before the wrapped st, W&T. **Sizes 49, 53, 57, 61, 65:** repeat the last two rows once more. Turn and knit across all sts, picking up wrapped sts and knitting them together with the sts they wrap.

Break yarn and put shoulders on st holders or scrap yarn.

Back
Place Back sts back on needles, and attach yarn ready to begin a RS row. Work through Armhole shaping directions as done for front. 88 (98, 106, 110, 112, 126, 132, 142, 146) sts remain.

Work 23 (22, 24, 24, 24, 26, 28, 25, 25) rows in St st.

On the next RS row, sts are bound off at the back neck to form the neckline.

K 19 (24, 27, 28, 28, 32, 34, 41, 43) sts, BO the next 50 (50, 52, 54, 56, 62, 64, 60, 60) sts, then K to the end of row.

Turn and P to 2 sts before neckline edge of left shoulder; P2tog. Attach a new ball of yarn at the right shoulder; P2tog TBL across the first 2 sts, then P to end. 18 (23, 26, 27, 27, 31, 33, 40, 42) sts remain on each shoulder.

Work short rows as done for front, reversing right and left side directions, but do not break yarn.

Join Shoulders
Put front shoulder sts back on spare needles. Turn body inside out, and join the shoulders together using working yarn from the back and the Three-needle Bind-Off technique.

Finishing
Set in Sleeves
With right sides facing out, set sleeves into armhole openings, making sure that the center of each sleeve cap is placed at the shoulder seam and that the seam under the sleeve and bound off sts of the armhole are centered. Pin in place. Using yarn needle and yarn, begin at the underarm and sew sleeves into the armholes, using Mattress stitch.

Collar
The collar can be worked as a rolled crew neck or a turtleneck. For the crewneck, use smaller needles; for turtleneck, use the larger needles.

With RS facing and starting at right shoulder seam, PU and K 3 (3, 3, 3, 5, 5, 5, 5, 5) sts to the bound off sts at the back neck, 50 (50, 52, 54, 56, 62, 64, 60, 60) bound off sts across the neck, 3 (3, 3, 3, 5, 5, 5, 5, 5) sts up to the left shoulder seam, and 78 (76, 80, 82, 86, 94, 98, 90, 90) around front neckline edge back to right shoulder. 134 (132, 138, 142, 152, 166, 172, 160, 160) sts. PM and join to work in the round.

Crew Neck
Work in K1, P1 rib for 2". Break yarn, leaving a tail of several yards. Fold the collar towards the inside. Using the yarn tail, whipstitch the live sts to the back of the picked up row.

Turtleneck
Work in K1, P1 rib for 8-10", or until desired length, keeping in mind that the collar will be worn doubled. BO all sts very loosely.

Weave in ends. Wash and block to measurements.

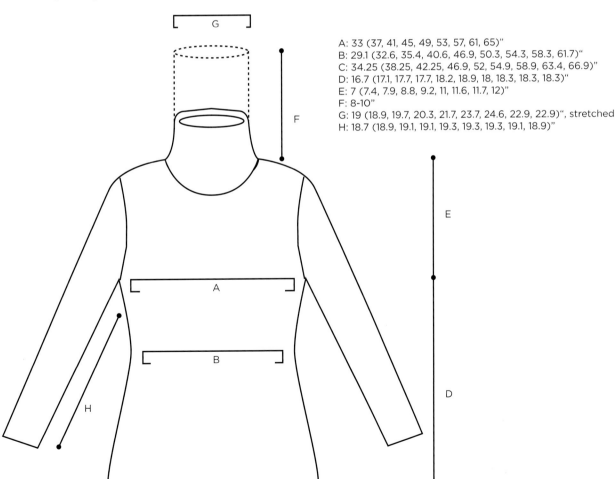

A: 33 (37, 41, 45, 49, 53, 57, 61, 65)"
B: 29.1 (32.6, 35.4, 40.6, 46.9, 50.3, 54.3, 58.3, 61.7)"
C: 34.25 (38.25, 42.25, 46.9, 52, 54.9, 58.9, 63.4, 66.9)"
D: 16.7 (17.1, 17.7, 17.7, 18.2, 18.9, 18, 18.3, 18.3, 18.3)"
E: 7 (7.4, 7.9, 8.8, 9.2, 11, 11.6, 11.7, 12)"
F: 8-10"
G: 19 (18.9, 19.7, 20.3, 21.7, 23.7, 24.6, 22.9, 22.9)", stretched
H: 18.7 (18.9, 19.1, 19.1, 19.3, 19.3, 19.3, 19.1, 18.9)"

Knitting Graph Paper

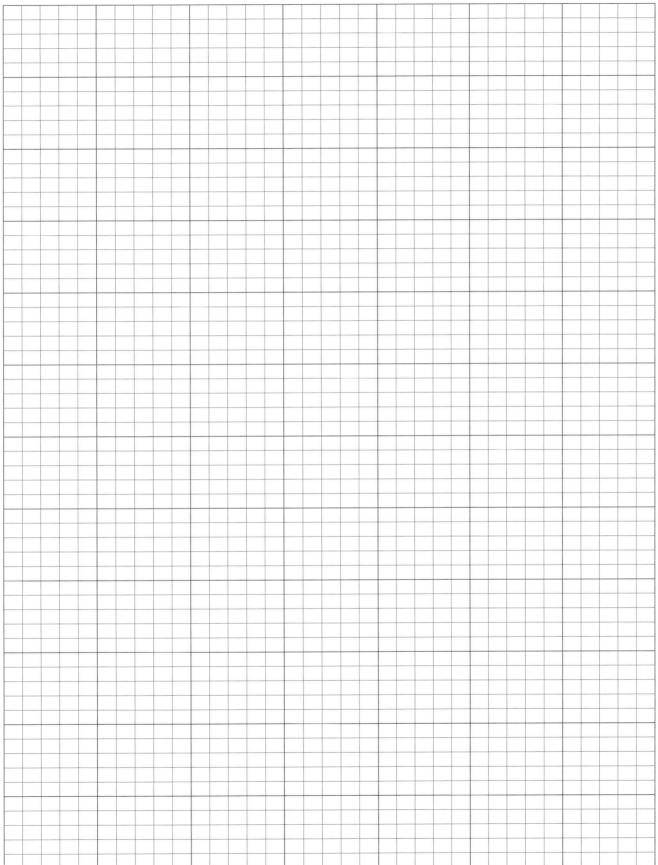

Knit Picks yarn is both luxe and affordable—a seeming contradiction trounced! But it's not just about the pretty colors; we also care deeply about fiber quality and fair labor practices, leaving you with a gorgeously reliable product you'll turn to time and time again.

This collection features

Stroll Hand Paint
Fingering Weight
75% Superwash Merino Wool, 25% Nylon

Stroll Tonal
Fingering Weight
75% Superwash Merino Wool, 25% Nylon

Stroll Glimmer
Fingering Weight
70% Superwash Merino Wool, 25% Nylon, 5% Stellina

Comfy
Fingering Weight
75% Pima Cotton, 25% Acrylic

Capretta
Fingering Weight
80% Superfine Merino Wool, 10% Cashmere, 10% Nylon

Stroll
Fingering Weight
75% Superwash Merino Wool, 25% Nylon

View these beautiful yarns and more at www.KnitPicks.com